To:
MARY ANN

From:
BABE & BARNEY

the ageless soul the ageless soul

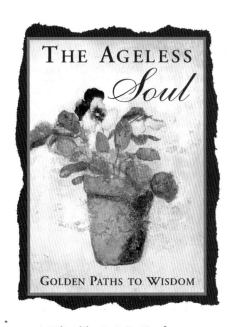

THE AGELESS
Soul

GOLDEN PATHS TO WISDOM

Edited by Lois L. Kaufman

Illustrated by Michael Clark

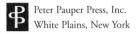

Peter Pauper Press, Inc.
White Plains, New York

Designed by Kerren Barbas

Illustrations copyright © 2000
Michael Clark
Licensed by Wild Apple Licensing

Text copyright © 2000
Peter Pauper Press, Inc.
202 Mamaroneck Avenue
White Plains, NY 10601
ISBN 0-88088-250-6
Printed in China
7 6 5 4 3 2 1

Visit us at www.peterpauper.com

THE AGELESS
Soul

GOLDEN PATHS TO WISDOM

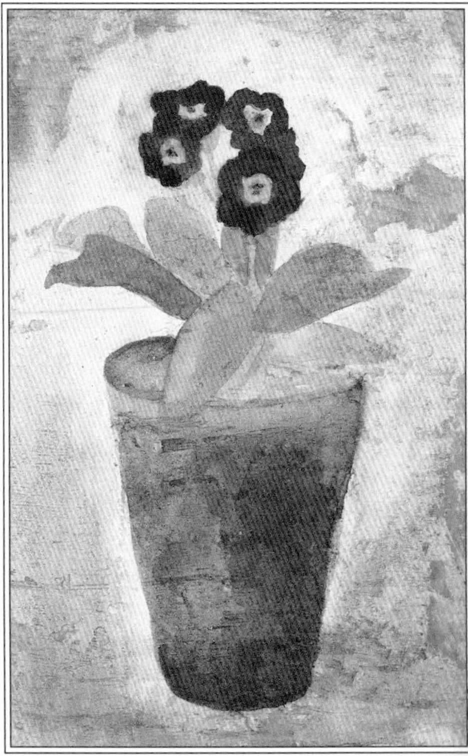

Introduction

Youth has its glory, but it is only as we begin to grow older that we can fully appreciate the fullness that life has to offer.

We have gained more freedom and flexibility, and the opportunity to venture into fields that perhaps never seemed to be available to us before. New perspectives bring new challenges, and new successes as well. We do not worry so much about failure, because we have learned to persevere.

This is the "daylight saving time" of life, the time to take advantage of every hour, and give meaning to every minute.

L. L. K.

*I*n youth we learn;
in age we understand.

MARIE VON EBNER ESCHENBACH

*O*ne thing is certain, and I have
always known it — the joys of my
life have nothing to do with age.

MAY SARTON

*K*eep your face
to the sunshine and you
cannot see the shadows.

HELEN KELLER

*Y*our vision will become
clear only when you look into
your heart. He who looks outside
dreams. He who looks
inside awakens.

CARL JUNG

*A*ge puzzles me.
I thought it was a quiet time.
My seventies were interesting
and fairly serene, but my
eighties are passionate.
I grow more intense as I age.

FLORIDA SCOTT-MAXWELL

*L*ife has got to be lived—
that's all there is to it. At seventy,
I would say the advantage is that
you take life more calmly. You
know that this, too, shall pass!

ELEANOR ROOSEVELT

*M*ost human beings today
waste some twenty-five to thirty
years of their lives before they
break through the actual and
conventional lies
which surround them.

ISADORA DUNCAN

Life is a series of experiences,
each of which makes us bigger,
even though it is hard to realize this.
For the world was built to
develop character, and we must
learn that the setbacks and griefs
which we endure help us
in our marching onward.

HENRY FORD

The young sow wild oats.
The old grow sage.

WINSTON CHURCHILL

A life making mistakes is
not only more honorable, but
more useful than a life spent
doing nothing at all.

GEORGE BERNARD SHAW

*P*atience and perseverance have a
magical effect before which difficulties disappear and obstacles vanish.

JOHN QUINCY ADAMS

*I*t takes a lot of time to be a
genius, you have to sit around
so much doing nothing,
really doing nothing.

GERTRUDE STEIN

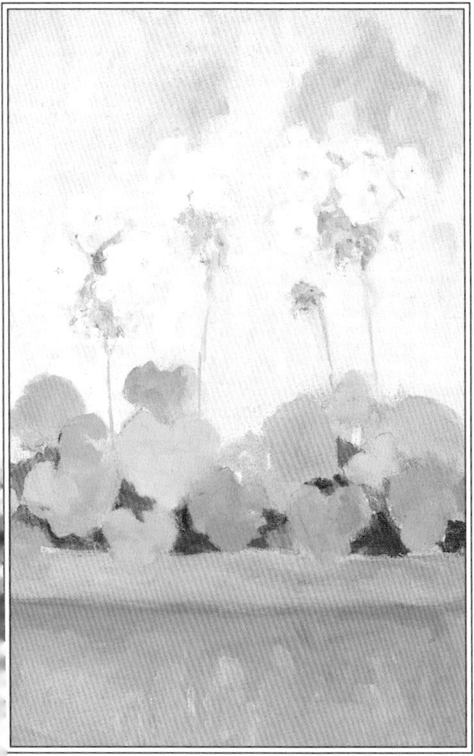

*O*nce you have been
confronted with a life-and-death
situation, trivia no longer matters.
Your perspective grows and
you live at a deeper level.
There's no time for pettiness.

<small>MARGARETTA (HAPPY) ROCKEFELLER</small>

*W*hat the caterpillar calls
the end of the world the
master calls a butterfly.

<small>RICHARD BACH</small>

The universe is change;
our life is what our
thoughts make it.

MARCUS AURELIUS

Develop an interest
in life as you see it; the people,
things, literature, music —
the world is so rich, simply
throbbing with rich treasures,
beautiful souls and interesting
people. Forget yourself.

HENRY MILLER

I'm in a very enviable
position, being able to work like
this forty-five years later.
It's always beginning!
I never have a sense of finishing
up, just new things beginning.
When I die, they're going to
carry me off a stage.

ANGELA LANSBURY

*A*t fifty, I think I may
be growing up at last.

ALI MCGRAW

*P*eople get happier
as they get older. A big chunk
of that happiness comes
from passing the decision-making
hurdles of youth, such as whether
you should marry, have kids, take
that job or buy a new house.
Now you're reaping the rewards
of whatever decisions you
made in the past.

WALTER S. SMITSON, PH.D.

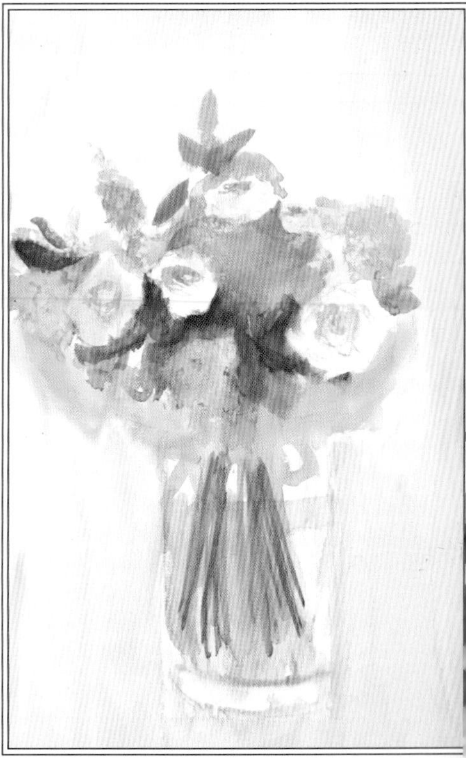

*I*t's exciting to get old, with
a body that still functions, though
these days my spirit is doing most
of the work. The early and middle
experiences of your life take
on a greater reality with age,
and you gain an overview.

BARBARA MORGAN, *AT AGE 83*

*T*he process of maturing is an
art to be learned, an effort to be
sustained. By the age of fifty you
have made yourself what you are,
and if it is good, it is better
than your youth.

MARYA MANNES

*D*on't wait for your ship to
come in, and feel angry and
cheated when it doesn't.
Get going with something small.

IRENE KASSORLA

*T*he voyage of discovery
lies not in finding new landscapes,
but in having new eyes.

MARCEL PROUST

*H*ave courage and a
little willingness to venture
and be defeated.

ROBERT FROST

*E*very now and then somebody
asks me when I'm going to retire.
Retire?... I will always be leading
the cheers for life, and I hope
that's the way people will always
see me and remember me, as a
cheerleader for life, out there in
front of the crowd with a
megaphone in my hand, crying out,
Gimme an L! Gimme an I!
Gimme an F! Gimme an E!
LIFE! LIFE! LIFE!

MICKEY ROONEY

*L*ife is what we make it,
always has been, always will be.

GRANDMA MOSES

The last 100 years of my life have
been filled with new things.

LILLIAN POSTMAN, *AT AGE 108*

I would rather be ashes than dust!
I would rather that my spark
should burn out in a brilliant blaze
than it should be stifled by dry rot.
I would rather be a superb meteor,
every atom of me in magnificent
glow, than a sleepy and permanent
planet. The proper function of man
is to live, not to exist. I shall not
waste my days in trying to
prolong them; I shall use my time.

JACK LONDON

To me, old age is always
fifteen years older than I am.

BERNARD BARUCH

I always say my God will take
care of me. If it's my time I'll go,
and if it's not I won't. I feel that
He really has a lot of important
things for me to do. And He's
going to make sure that
I'm here to do them.

JOYCELYN ELDERS

A man is not old as long
as he is seeking something.

JEAN ROSTAND

If wrinkles must be written
upon our brows, let them not
be written upon the heart.
The spirit should never grow old.

JAMES A. GARFIELD

Age does not protect you
from love. But love, to some
extent, protects you from age.

JEANNE MOREAU

You don't get to choose
how you're going to die, or
when. You can only decide how
you're going to live now.

JOAN BAEZ

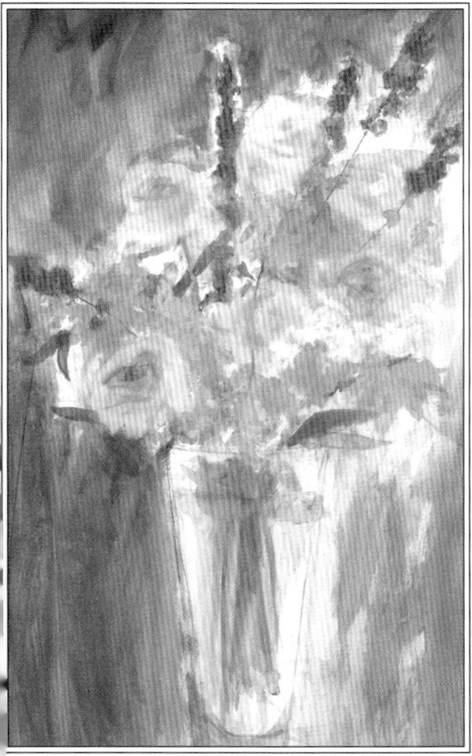

For the ignorant,
old age is as winter;
for the learned, it is a harvest.

HASIDIC SAYING

Far away there in the sunshine
are my highest aspirations.
I may not reach them, but I can
look up and see their beauty,
believe in them and try to follow
where they may lead.

LOUISA MAY ALCOTT

*L*et me not forget that I am the daughter of a woman who bent her head, trembling, between the blades of a cactus, her wrinkled face full of ecstasy over the promise of a flower, a woman who herself never ceased to flower, untiringly, during three quarters of a century.

COLETTE

*T*here is absolutely no reason you can't feel as well as you did at fifty, and the secret is never to stop working.

DAVID BROWN,
FILM PRODUCER, AT AGE 71

When we long for life
without difficulties, remind us that
oaks grow strong in contrary
winds and diamonds
are made under pressure.

PETER MARSHALL

Don't be afraid your life will end;
be afraid that it will never begin.

GRACE HANSEN

I never feel age. . . .
If you have creative work,
you don't have age or time.

LOUISE NEVELSON

*P*erhaps middle age is,
or should be, a period of
shedding shells; the shell of
ambition, the shell of material
accumulations and possessions,
the shell of the ego.

ANNE MORROW LINDBERGH,
GIFT FROM THE SEA

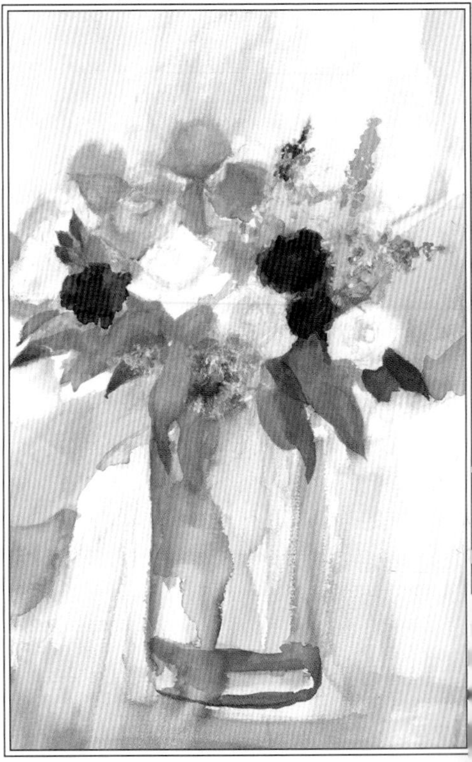

*Y*outh is not a time of life;
it is a state of mind.
People grow old only by
deserting their ideals and by
outgrowing the consciousness of
youth. . . . The way to keep
young is to keep your faith
young. Keep your self-confidence
young. Keep your hope young.

LUELLA F. PHELAN

$\mathcal{D}$o not follow
where the path may lead.
Go instead where there is no
path and leave a trail.

MURIEL STRODE

$\mathcal{N}$othing can help us face
the unknown future with more
courage and optimism than
remembering the glory moments,
and everybody has a few of them.

EDA LeSHAN

*T*he secret to brandy is age.
The secret to everything is age.

LINE SPOKEN BY ANTHONY QUINN
IN THE MOVIE
A WALK IN THE CLOUDS

*O*ne of the signs
of passing youth is the birth
of a sense of fellowship with other
human beings as we take
our place among them.

VIRGINIA WOOLF

I'M NOT YOUNG ANY MORE, AND

It's time for *me*.

I feel wiser.

I feel calmer, more at peace with myself and the world.

I count my blessings.

I'm more open to new experiences.

I value being comfortable.

I have fewer delusions.

I'm less concerned with what other people think.

I can make choices.

I'm free, I can *fly!*

It's really
about my own life.
I have to wrestle because I am
too much taken with life.
That's my philosophy:
Keep fighting for life
and God will beautifully reveal
his face to you because you
have not given up
and are going into death
on the wave of life.

GIAN CARLO MENOTTI,
ABOUT HIS OPERA JACOB'S PRAYER

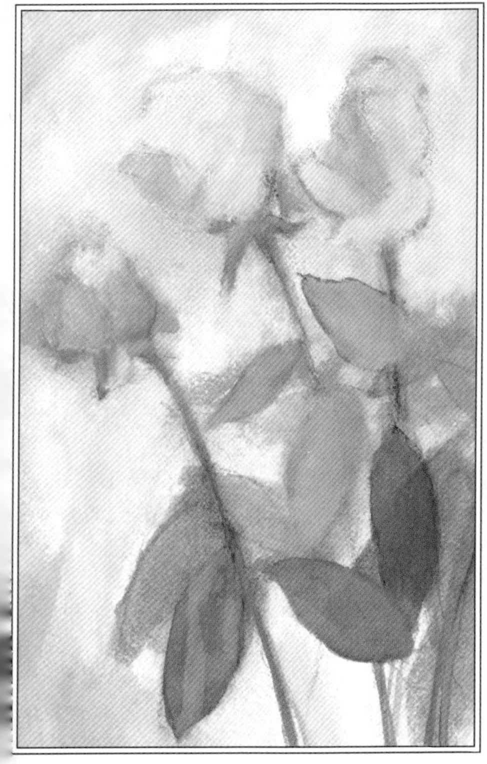

If I knew I were going to die tomorrow, I'd think, so soon? Still, if a man has spent his life doing what he wanted to do, he ought to be able to say goodbye without regrets.

PAUL BOWLES

When you look the way I do, why not brag.

JUNE LOCKHART, *AT 70*

*P*lease don't retouch my
wrinkles; it took me so
long to earn them.

ANNA MAGNANI,
WHO DIDN'T WANT THE STUDIO STILLS FOR
THE ROSE TATTOO *AIRBRUSHED*

*T*he secret of eternal youth
is arrested development.

ALICE ROOSEVELT LONGWORTH

$\mathcal{I}$m not worried about getting older because I'm getting better. I can hold a note longer, I can sing a song better. At 50, you know a lot about yourself and I feel I can teach people important things about getting to this stage in life . . . Hopefully, you'll see me rockin' and rollin' at 105!

PATTI LABELLE

A man over ninety
is a great comfort to all his
elderly neighbors: he is a
picket-guard at the extreme
outpost; and the young folks of
sixty and seventy feel that the
enemy must get by him before he
can come near their camp.

OLIVER WENDELL HOLMES

*P*eople's expectations of age
have changed a great deal. . . .
There's a certain inner flexibility.
People no longer feel
that at 50 it's all over.

ALICE ADAMS

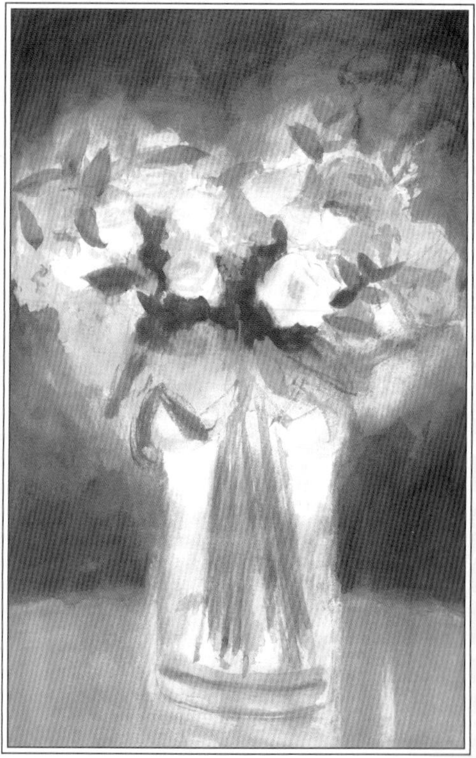

*Y*outh, large, lusty, loving—
youth full of grace, force,
fascination, Do you know that
Old Age may come after you with
equal grace, force, fascination?

WALT WHITMAN

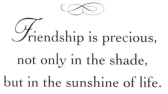

*Y*ou have to invent and
reinvent yourself. I keep reinvent-
ing myself as I grow. I take more
chances and stick my neck out...

GEORGETTE MOSBACHER

*F*riendship is precious,
not only in the shade,
but in the sunshine of life.

THOMAS JEFFERSON

$\mathcal{S}$ure, you've made mistakes, you have some pains, but you become more and more whole… you're not driven by things like you were when you were younger. You can take risks in new ways. It's a subtle thing. You can show more of the reality of yourself instead of hiding behind a mask for fear of revealing too much.

BETTY FRIEDAN

It is not how old you are,
but how you are old.

MARIE DRESSLER

*S*ure, I'm for helping the elderly.
I'm going to be old myself someday.

LILLIAN CARTER, *AT AGE 85*

*S*uccess is having a flair
for the thing that you are doing,
knowing that is not enough,
that you have got to have hard
work and a sense of purpose.

MARGARET THATCHER

*L*et's face it:
mandatory retirement is a terrible
idea. I've always felt it was
ridiculous that when a guy
reaches sixty-five, no matter what
shape he's in, we retire him
instantly. We should be depending
on our older executives.
They have the experience.
They have the wisdom.

LEE IACOCCA

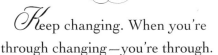

*K*eep changing. When you're
through changing—you're through.

BRUCE BARTON

$\mathcal{L}$ive all you can; it is a mistake
not to. It doesn't matter so much
what you do in particular, so
long as you have your life.
If you haven't had that,
what have you had?

HENRY JAMES

$\mathcal{I}$ could not, at any age,
be content to take my place by
the fireside and simply look on.
Life was meant to be lived, and
curiosity must be kept alive. One
must never, for whatever reason,
turn his back on life.

ELEANOR ROOSEVELT

I have enjoyed greatly the second blooming that comes when you finish the life of the emotions and of personal relations; and suddenly find — at the age of fifty, say — that a whole new life has opened before you, filled with things you can think about, study, or read about. . . . It is as if a fresh sap of ideas and thoughts was rising in you.

AGATHA CHRISTIE

In the depth of winter, I finally learned that within me there lay an invincible summer.

ALBERT CAMUS

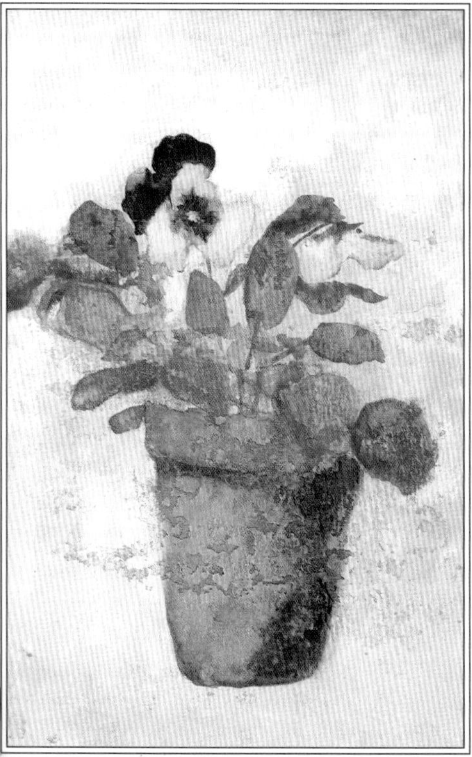

$\mathcal{A}$ge to me means nothing. I can't get old; I'm working. I was old when I was twenty-one and out of work. As long as you're working, you stay young. When I'm in front of an audience, all that love and vitality sweeps over me and I forget my age.

GEORGE BURNS

$\mathcal{J}$ust don't give up trying to do what you really want to do. Where there is love and inspiration, I don't think you can go wrong.

ELLA FITZGERALD

$\mathcal{L}$ife is like riding a bicycle; you don't fall off unless you stop pedaling.

CLAUDE PEPPER

$\mathcal{Y}$ou must learn day by day, year by year, to broaden your horizon. The more things you love, the more you are interested in, the more you enjoy, the more you are indignant about, the more you have left when anything happens.

ETHEL BARRYMORE

$\mathcal{T}$he greatest use of life is to spend it for something that will outlast it.

WILLIAM JAMES

*A*dvise those old fellows of ours to follow my example; keep up your spirits, and that will keep up your bodies; you will no more stoop under the weight of age than if you had swallowed a handspike.

BENJAMIN FRANKLIN

*N*o age or time of life, no position or circumstance, has a monopoly on success. Any age is the right age to start doing!

GERARD

*W*e are always the same age inside.

GERTRUDE STEIN

*F*or me life is a challenge.
And it will be a challenge if I live
to be a hundred or if
I get to be a trillionaire.

BEAH RICHARDS

*S*ecurity is mostly
a superstition. It does not exist in
nature, nor do the children of
men as a whole experience it.
Avoiding danger is no safer in the
long run than outright exposure.
Life is either a daring adventure
or nothing at all.

HELEN KELLER

$\mathcal{I}$ am not going to let a box camera, now an antique, or any thing or person tell me whether or not I am an antique. I will decide, and I'm not ready yet.

My idea of an antique is that it has to be at least 150 years old, which gives me a little breather.

EDA LeShan

$\mathcal{I}$t's only when we truly know and understand that we have a limited time on earth—and that we have no way of knowing when our time is up—that we will begin to live each day to the fullest, as if it was the only one we had.

ELISABETH KÜBLER-ROSS

*T*wenty years from now
you will be more disappointed by
the things you didn't do than by
the ones you did do. So throw off
the bowlines. Sail away from the
safe harbor. Catch the trade
winds in your sails.
Explore. Dream. Discover.

MARK TWAIN

I guess at my age I should
feel a little older, but I don't . . .
My body still feels like it wants to
run in the park.

LENA HORNE, *AT AGE 67*

*T*here's a lot of talk about
self-esteem these days. It seems
pretty basic to me. If you want to
feel proud of yourself, you've got
to do things you can be proud of.
Feelings follow actions.

OSEOLA MCCARTY,
*WASHERWOMAN WHO, LATE IN LIFE, GAVE ALL HER
SAVINGS TO A SCHOLARSHIP FUND*

*T*oo often people
set their lives by the calendar.
It takes all the fun out of life.

JOHN GLENN,
AFTER HIS LATEST SHUTTLE MISSION

$\mathcal{I}$t is an accepted myth that when people grow older they fall apart and don't do anything. I don't think that is altogether true. I think it is absolutely up to the individual. I mean, if you feel over the hill, you are over the hill. Each of us must do whatever we have a passion to do. It is our decision.

JESSICA TANDY

$\mathcal{A}$ll growth is a leap in the dark, a spontaneous, unpremeditated act without benefit of experience.

HENRY MILLER

$\mathcal{T}$here seems to be a connection between being useful and productive and how long you live. Living a 52-week-a-year vacation isn't what older people want. They want purpose.

DAVID WOLFE,
CONSUMER BEHAVIOR CONSULTANT

Life isn't a matter of milestones but of moments.

ROSE FITZGERALD KENNEDY

Through perseverance many people win success out of what seemed destined to be certain failure.

BENJAMIN DISRAELI

Conscious aging is saying that the big adventure is the inner journey, and that does not have to stop when you no longer ski downhill.

RICK MOODY

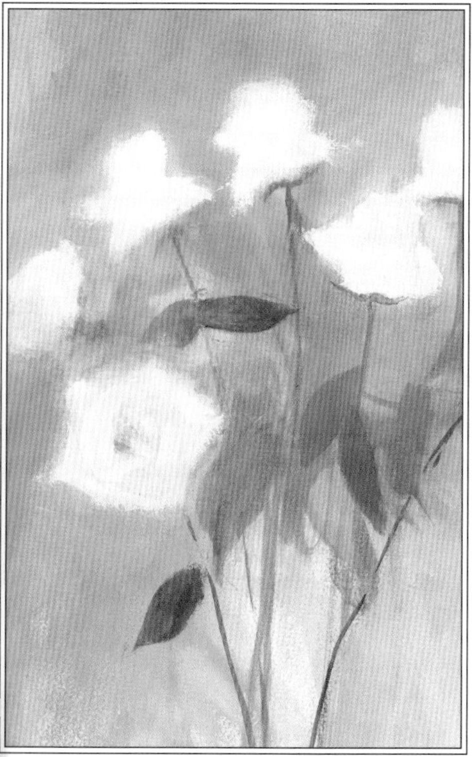

$\mathcal{M}$ost of the important things in the world have been accomplished by people who have kept on trying when there seemed to be no hope at all.

DALE CARNEGIE

$\mathcal{Y}$ou have a revolution among senior workers who are rejecting the stereotypes and saying: "Wait a minute, I'm not done yet."

KEN DYCHTWALD

$\mathcal{S}$ixty-five percent (61 percent of retirees, 70 percent of nonretirees) said it is "a time to begin a new chapter by being active and involved, starting new activities and setting new goals."

MARC FREEDMAN,
FROM A NATIONWIDE SURVEY ON RETIREMENT ATTITUDES

$\mathcal{L}$earn to see, and then you'll know there is no end to the new worlds of our vision.

CARLOS CASTANEDA

$\mathscr{I}$ postpone death by living,
by suffering, by error, by risking,
by giving, by losing.

ANAÏS NIN

$\mathscr{S}$ecurity is not the meaning
of my life. Great opportunities
are worth the risk.

SHIRLEY HUFSTEDLER

$\mathscr{T}$he world is round, and the
place which may seem like the
end may also be the beginning.

IVY BAKER PRIEST

*Y*es, of course [this age] is materialistic, but the only way to counteract it is to create spiritual things. Don't worry yourself about the materialism too much. Create and stir other people to create!

ROBERT FROST

*T*here is a fountain of youth: it is your mind, your talents, the creativity you bring to your life and the lives of the people you love. When you learn to tap this source, you will truly have defeated age.

SOPHIA LOREN

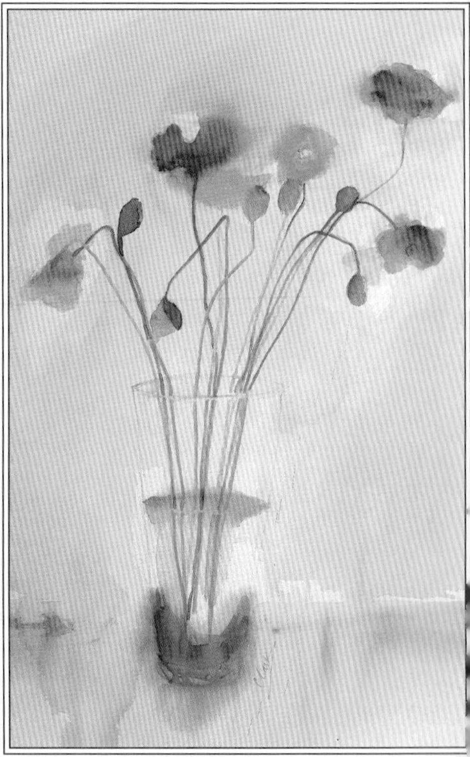

the ageless soul the ageless soul
geless soul the ageless soul the
ss soul the ageless soul the a
the ageless soul the ageless sou
geless soul the ageless soul th
ss soul the ageless soul the a
the ageless soul the ageless sou
geless soul the ageless soul th
ss soul the ageless soul the a
the ageless soul the ageless so
geless soul the ageless soul th
ss soul the ageless soul the a
the ageless soul the ageless so